GW00733396

Stories by Maureen Spurgeon

This edition first published 2002 by Brown Watson
The Old Mill, 76 Fleckney Road,
Kibworth Beauchamp, Leics LE8 0HG

ISBN: 0-7097-1501-3

Printed in the E.U

Now I Can READ

A Collection of Two Minute Tales

Brown Watson
ENGLAND

CONTENTS

WHERE IS THE LOST CHICK?

Hetty Hen was counting her chicks. 'One, two, three, four, five, six! All my chicks are here!'

They went to the yard.

'One, two, three, four, five,' counted Hetty. 'Where is chick number six?'

'We went to the duck pond,' said the first chick. So, off they went.

'I have lost a chick!' said Hetty.

'We shall look for it!' quacked Debbie Duck.

'We went to the farmhouse,' said the second chick.

'To see Kitten!' said the third. So, off they went. Five chicks and the ducks.

'I have lost a chick!' said Hetty.

'I shall look for it!' said Kitten.

'We went to the cowshed,' said the fourth chick. So, off they went. Five chicks, ducks and Kitten.

'I have lost a chick!' said Hetty.

'I shall look for it!' said Cora Cow.

'We went to the stable,' said the fifth chick. So, off they went. Five chicks, ducks, Kitten and Cora.

'I have lost a chick!' said Hetty.

'Let us go to the meadow!' said Hector.

So, off they went. Five chicks, ducks, Kitten, Cora Cow and Hector Horse.

Hetty looked around. 'One, two, three, four, five chicks, ducks, Kitten, Cora Cow, Hector Horse...'

'Cheep!' came a voice. 'Cheep! What about me, Mother Hen?'

'My lost chick!' cried Hetty. 'Where have you been?'

'Following you!' cheeped the cheeky chick. 'I think Follow My Leader is a LOVELY game!'

READ THESE WORDS AGAIN!

counting   lost

quacked   shall

first   off

second   fourth

fifth   voice

what   where

following   leader

14

WHAT CAN YOU SEE HERE?

duck pond

cow

six chicks

stable

Kitten

FOOD FOR A PARTY

Teena Bear was having a party at Honeypot Cottage! Teddy had helped Daddy to make cheese rolls. 'Here comes Wood-Cutter Bear!' cried Daddy. 'We can take all these on his handcart!'

'Do not forget my milk shakes!' said Mummy. She fetched some big jugs, each with a lid on top.

Soon, they met Gardener Bear. She was bringing lots of salad.

'Lovely!' said Teddy. 'I LOVE salad sandwiches!'

Next, they met Baker Bear. She had made cakes and jam tarts for the party. Wood-Cutter Bear put them all on his cart.

'Let us call for Woody!' he said. But when they reached Woody's caravan, all was quiet.

'Ssh!' said Woody. 'See those rabbits? I think they are lost! And I have no food for them!'

'What about some salad?' said Gardener Bear. She took some from the cart.

Just then, some squirrels appeared.

'They look hungry to me!' said Teddy. 'Do they like cheese rolls?'

'Give some cake to these poor gulls!' said Baker Bear. 'When they fly inland, it is because there is bad weather at sea!'

When they got to Honeypot Cottage, Teena was at the gate.

'I AM glad to see you, Mummy Bear!' she cried. 'Can you spare some milk shake for this kitten?'

Teena did not understand why everyone began to smile!

READ THESE WORDS AGAIN!

party	cheese
helped	rolls
salad	sandwiches
cart	quiet
reached	gardener
hungry	there
bad	weather

WHAT CAN YOU SEE HERE?

rabbits

squirrels

cottage

gulls

kitten

FOX AND THE PIE

One day, a fox crept into the farm.

'Go away!' barked Dinky Dog.

'Now, now!' purred Fox. 'I have only come to see you!'

'And to steal food!' said Dinky. She barked again.

The farmer's wife came out. 'Fox!' she cried, but Fox was already across the yard!

Soon, Fox saw Guppy Goat next to the wall. In his mouth was a big, tasty-looking pie, left over from a picnic.

'Hello, Guppy!' said Fox. 'My, what a tasty-looking pie!'

'Yes..' began Guppy. As he opened his mouth, out fell the pie! Fox snapped it up and ran off. What a feast for a hungry fox!

Along came Donny Donkey. 'Fox!' he brayed. 'What a tasty-looking pie!'

Fox nodded his head. He was smarter than Guppy!

'I saw another fox with a pie like that,' said Donny. 'But his was MUCH bigger!' Fox nearly opened his mouth in surprise! Donny led him to a stream.

'There he is!' said Donny. He nodded at the water. 'See that pie!'

Fox looked into the stream. Looking up at him was another fox with a big pie in his mouth!

Fox gave a growl. SPLASH! His pie fell into the stream. Fox growled again, this time with rage!

'Still up to your tricks, Fox?' shouted the farmer's wife, and she chased him away with a broom.

And the pie? By the time Donny fished it out, it was already soggy, but it was just as tasty as it looked!

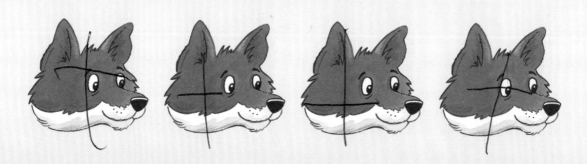

READ THESE WORDS AGAIN!

crept	barked
steal	purred
yard	mouth
snapped	opened
surprise	growl
splash	rage
already	soggy

WHAT CAN YOU SEE HERE?

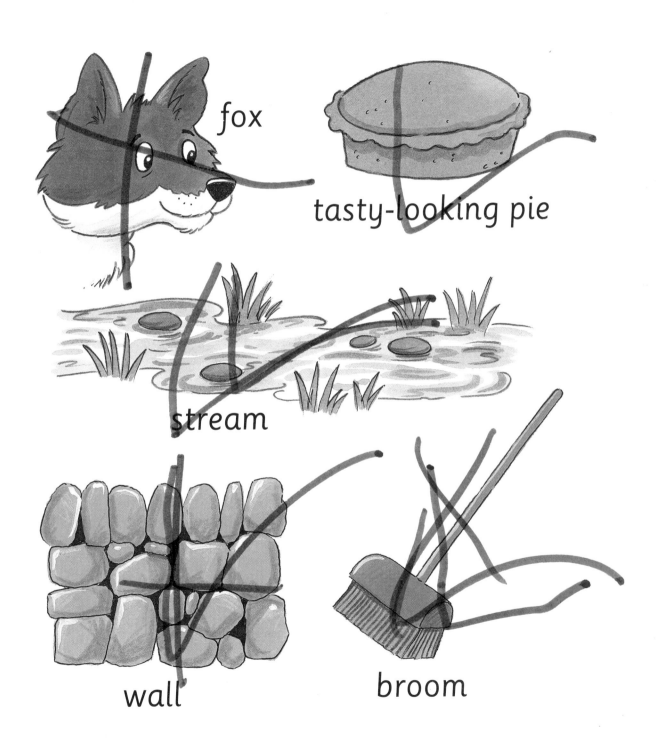

fox

tasty-looking pie

stream

wall

broom

DADDY AND THE SCHOOL FAIR

There was going to be a School Fair to raise money for some new toys. What ideas everyone had!

'Skittles!' said Teddy Bear.

'Coconut shy!' said Bella Bear.

'Egg and spoon races!' cried Billy Bear. 'And lucky dips!'

Teddy told Mummy Bear all about it. 'Good idea!' she said. 'We can make cakes to sell!'

Daddy Bear took off his reading glasses. 'You also buy too many things at school fairs!' he said.

'I do NOT!' said Mummy. 'You spend money, too!'

Daddy shut his book. 'I help in other ways!' he said. 'Teddy, help me pack some books to sell!'

Lots of bears came to the Fair. 'I must buy some cakes,' said Mummy.

'But, Mummy,' said Teddy, 'WE made lots of cakes to sell!'

'Yes,' she said, 'but I like the cakes baked by Baker Bear!'

Suddenly Daddy Bear gave a shout, and rushed over to the book stall.

'I left my glasses in that box of books by mistake!' he told Teacher Bear. 'Here they are, inside this book!'

'If you want that book,' said Teacher Bear, 'you must buy it!'

'Yes, yes!' said Daddy. He was glad to have his glasses back! 'We must raise money for the school!'

'Fancy buying your own book, Daddy!' smiled Teddy. 'I wonder what you are going to buy next?'

'Ice creams!' said Daddy. 'I wonder who wants one?'

READ THESE WORDS AGAIN!

fair	raise
money	new
toys	ideas
reading	glasses
other	suddenly
shout	rushed
inside	wonder

WHAT CAN YOU SEE HERE?

skittles

coconut shy

books

lucky dip

ice cream

GUPPY THE GOAT

'What use is Guppy Goat?' said Hector Horse. 'What does he do?'

'He does not give milk,' said Cora Cow.

'He does not lay eggs,' said Hetty Hen.

'He is useless!' said Hector.

'Guppy IS nice!' said Donny Donkey. But nobody listened.

'They say I am useless!' Guppy told Kitten. 'All except Donny!'

'They do not mean it!' said Kitten. 'Cheer up, Guppy!'

Just then, Guppy saw that a gate had been left open. He bent down and slipped one horn under the latch. Then he pushed the gate shut and let the latch fall.

Next, he saw some paper on the ground. He used his horns to pick up the paper and put the bits in a bin. He stuck one horn into a tin can which had been thrown into a tree. That went into the bin, too.

Then, some boys began chasing sheep! How Guppy chased those boys away!

The sheep bleated in fright. One got caught on a wire fence. But Guppy nibbled and chewed at the sheep's wool until it was free.

'Thank you, Guppy!' said the farmer. 'Kitten said you closed the gate, you picked up all the litter and you chased those boys away! Now you have saved a sheep! You work so hard on our farm!'

And when they heard all that Guppy had done, the other animals had to agree! Clever old Guppy!

READ THESE WORDS AGAIN!

what	useless
listened	except
cheer	slipped
horn	pushed
ground	saved
work	hard
other	agree

WHAT CAN YOU SEE HERE?

gate

latch

Guppy
Goat

litter

boys

TEDDY AND THE WISHING WELL

It had been hot for a long time in Teddy Town. 'We have hardly any water!' said Policeman Bear.

'No water?' said Teddy. 'But what about our paddling pool?'

'What about my crops?' said Farmer Bear. 'I have even used up the water in my old well!'

'A well,' Teddy said to himself. 'Just the thing!' He found some bricks and set to work.

'Hello, Teddy!' called Barry Bear. 'What are you doing?'

'Making a well,' said Teddy.

'You need cement,' said Barry. 'I will go and fetch some.'

By the time he came back, Teddy had set the bricks in a circle on the ground.

'Well done!' smiled Barry.

They stuck the bricks together. Then they fixed sticks at the side of the well and tied a bucket on a rope.

'You cannot get water from that well, Teddy!' cried Policeman Bear, laughing.

'A well must be sunk deep into the earth to draw water from the ground!'

'It can be a wishing well,' said Teacher Bear. 'Let us wish!'

Nobody said what they wished, but next day, Farmer Bear's crops grew fresh and green and birds splashed in a puddle. There was even water in the wishing well! Everyone agreed, rain was needed just as much as sunshine.

'And we got our wish, Barry!' cried Teddy. 'Well, well!'

READ THESE WORDS AGAIN!

water	paddling
crops	bricks
cement	circle
fixed	sticks
laughing	earth
ground	nobody
splashed	sunshine

WHAT CAN YOU SEE HERE?

Teddy

puddle

Policeman Bear

Farmer Bear

wishing well

A BELL FOR CORA COW

Cora Cow won a gold bell at a show! 'I shall wear it on a ribbon all the time!' she said.

'You must take it off when you eat,' said Dinky Dog.

'And when you sleep!' said Pixie Puppy.

'Then I may lose it!' said Cora. 'No! I shall not take it off!'

Cora went to the meadow, the bell tinkling and jingling. She sat in the shade of a tree and closed her eyes. The bell tinkled. She moved her head.

The bell jingled. She stood up. The bell tinkled. 'I shall go to the stream and have a drink!' she said.

At the stream she bent her head towards the cool water. The bell slipped down in front of her face, tinkling and jingling. Whatever she did, the bell got in the way.

So, Cora went to find some grass to eat, the bell still tinkling. She bent down. The bell tinkled and jingled. She tried moving her head. But, she could not move!

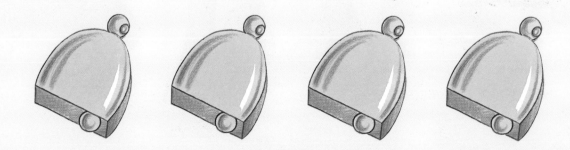

'Moo!' cried Cora, her bell tinkling even louder. 'Help me!'

'Your ribbon has caught on the bush!' said the farmer. 'I will cut you free with my scissors!'

Cora said nothing. Her poor neck felt so stiff and sore.

'Your bell is a bit dented,' said the farmer. 'But it still jingles. Shall we hang it up in the cow shed?' Cora nodded. How nice it was not to have the tinkling and jingling of the bell around her neck!

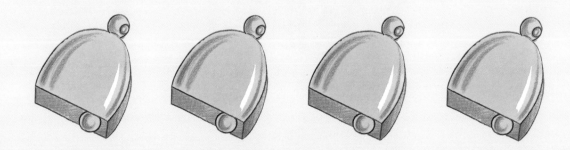

READ THESE WORDS AGAIN!

gold tinkling

jingling shade

moved head

front face

whatever find

some tried

caught stiff

WHAT CAN YOU SEE HERE?

bell

ribbon

tree

grass

scissors

BRIAN BEAR AND THE CAKE

Brian Bear had made a big cake to share with his friends. 'It looks a bit plain to me,' he told Teddy.

'We can make some icing,' said Teddy. 'And chocolate spread!'

Brian went to fetch the things from the kitchen. On the wall was a picture of Bella with Jolly Clown. 'A clown cake!' he cried. 'That is an idea!'

He began cutting bits off the cake. An oblong for the body and a round shape for the head!

Then a bit to make a hat! He rolled out some marzipan to make hair for the clown and Teddy made a marzipan jacket.

'He can have chocolate boots,' said Brian, 'chocolate eyes, a chocolate nose and a big icing sugar smile! What a cake!'

'It is a bit small, now,' said Teddy, 'and we made too much marzipan and chocolate spread.'

Just then, there was a ring at the door. There was no time to make anything else!

'Brian!' cried Bella. 'You and Teddy HAVE been busy!'

'All these lovely little cakes!' said Teena. She tasted a piece that had been cut off.

'Mmm..! Try a marzipan dip!' said Woody. He put some on his bit of cake. 'Scrummy!'

'And this chocolate dip!' said Billy. 'Mmmm, yummy!'

'What about our clown cake?' asked Brian.

'That looks lovely!' said Teena. 'MUCH too good to eat!'

READ THESE WORDS AGAIN!

cake   friends

chocolate   spread

kitchen   clown

oblong   round

shape   hair

sugar   anything

piece   lovely

WHAT CAN YOU SEE HERE?

marzipan

icing

jacket

picture

boots

DONNY COUNTS UP!

There was going to be a birthday party for Pixie Puppy!

'Carrots for Hector Horse!' said Dinky Dog, emptying a sack. 'Corn for Hetty Hen. Bran for Peggy Pig. How many dishes do we need, Donny Donkey?'

'Hetty Hen, one,' began Donny. 'Hector Horse, two. Billy Goat, three. Guppy Goat, four. Kitty Cat, five. Cora Cow, six. Peggy Pig, seven. And you, Dinky! Eight!'

'No!' said Dinky. 'Count again!'

So Donny counted. 'Hetty Hen, one. Hector Horse, two. Billy Goat, three. Guppy Goat, four. Kitty Cat, five. Cora Cow, six. Peggy Pig, seven. Dinky, eight and – I forgot Pixie! Nine!'

'Is that right?' asked Dinky.

'Yes!' cried Donny. 'That IS right!'

'Right!' said Dinky. 'You can put the dishes out!' So Donny began.

'Hetty Hen, one. Hector Horse, two. Billy Goat, three. Guppy Goat, four. Kitty Cat, five. Cora Cow, six. Peggy Pig, seven. Dinky, eight. Pixie, nine.'

Donny stopped. 'What about ME?' he said.

'You forgot to count yourself!' said Dinky. 'NOW count again!'

So Donny counted. 'Hetty Hen, one. Hector Horse, two. Billy Goat, three. Guppy Goat, four. Kitty cat, five. Cora Cow, six. Peggy Pig, seven. Dinky, eight. Pixie, nine, and ME, makes TEN!'

'Right!' said Donny. 'Now let us go and find the others and Pixie Puppy can have a LOVELY birthday party!'

READ THESE WORDS AGAIN!

birthday   party

carrots   emptying

dishes   one

two   count

again   forgot

right   eight

puppy   lovely

WHO CAN YOU SEE HERE?

Dinky Dog

Hetty Hen

Donny Donkey

Guppy Goat

Pixie Puppy

POOR JOLLY CLOWN!

Bella Bear was very upset.

'Look at Jolly Clown!' she said to Teddy. 'I lost him in the park! By the time Busy Bear found him, he was like this!'

Poor Jolly Clown! His hair had come out and his face was faded. Even his jolly smile had gone.

'Let us go and see Toy-Mender Bear!' said Teddy. 'He can make toys as good as new!'

'Poor Jolly Clown!' said Toy-Mender Bear. 'I shall do my best to fix him.'

Next day Bella told Teddy, 'I cannot wait any longer. I want to go and see Toy-Mender today! I must see if Jolly is better!'

When they got to Toy-Mender Bear's workshop, the door was open.

'I cannot mend this old thing!' he was saying. 'See his broken face? His paint is worn. His hands are crooked. I was going to put him in the bin!'

'You cannot put Jolly Clown in the bin!' yelled Bella loudly. 'If you cannot mend him, I shall take him home with me!'

'Who said I cannot mend Jolly Clown?' asked Toy-Mender Bear. 'I was telling Clock-Mender Bear about my old grandfather clock! Jolly is much better!' he added. 'He can go home tomorrow!'

Bella looked at Jolly Clown. His paint gleamed. His eyes shone. His smile was as wide as ever.

'Thank you, Toy-Mender Bear!' she said.

And, even the grandfather clock seemed to wink.

READ THESE WORDS AGAIN!

upset	found
hair	faded
smile	broken
face	worn
crooked	tomorrow
gleamed	eyes
smile	even

WHAT CAN YOU SEE HERE?

Bella Bear

Jolly Clown

Toy-Mender
Bear

grandfather
clock

Clock-Mender Bear

LETTY LAMB GETS A FRIGHT

Letty Lamb was always frightened!

'Baa!' she went as a leaf rustled. 'That frightened me. Baa!' she bleated at Kitten. 'You DID give me a fright!'

'No need to get frightened!' said Dinky Dog. But it was no use.

One hot afternoon, there was a distant rumble of thunder.

'Baa!' cried Letty. 'A storm! Storms frighten me! I must hide!'

Letty was frightened and ran inside an old barn.

Outside, the lightning flashed and thunder crashed overhead.

'BAA!' said Letty as loud as she could. 'BAA! Help! Help!'

There was a loud CRACK and then a CRASH! A big hole appeared in the roof. She could see the lightning flashing. The thunder got louder.

'Baa!' she bleated. 'Baa! BAA!'

'We are coming, Letty!' came the farmer's voice. 'A tree has crashed through the roof!'

The farmer and another man came inside the barn.

'Quick!' said the farmer. 'Cover all this hay to keep it dry! It is the winter feed for the animals!'

'Good thing we got here before it all got soaked!' said the man.

'Yes!' said the farmer. 'Thanks to brave Letty Lamb! She stayed here, bleating, until help came!'

'BAA!' said Letty. 'I am so ...' She stopped. Outside, lightning flashed and thunder crashed, but she was not frightened any more!

READ THESE WORDS AGAIN!

frightened	rustled
afternoon	thunder
storm	overhead
louder	crashed
hole	winter
feed	soaked
stayed	help

WHAT CAN YOU SEE HERE?

leaf

lightning

an old barn

roof

hay

THE MISSING STITCH

Kitty Bear never stopped knitting!

'What are you knitting, now?' asked Teddy.

'Socks and a scarf for Woody!' she said. 'Oh, I have dropped a stitch!'

'Where did she drop it, Teddy?' asked Billy. 'Did you see?'

'No,' said Teddy. 'We must see if we can find another one!'

Woody was in his garden.

'Ooh!' he gasped, rubbing his side. 'I have got a stitch!'

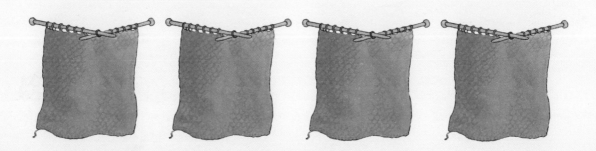

'A stitch?' cried Teddy. 'Is it the one Kitty Bear dropped?' But Woody had already gone indoors.

'So much mending!' somebody else was saying. 'All these things will need a lot of stitching!'

'Busy Bear!' cried Teddy. 'Woody had a stitch just now!'

'Woody?' said Busy Bear. 'Well, I did try to mend his pullover! But as fast as I stitched, the old stitches came undone...'

'We only need ONE stitch!' cried Billy Bear, pulling at the pullover.

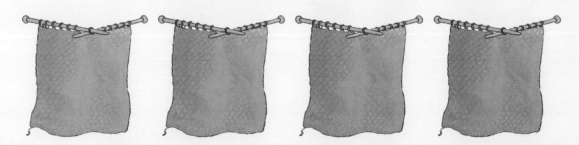

One stitch came undone. Then another and another. They ran back to Kitty with lots of undone stitches!

'Here is your stitch, Kitty!' said Teddy. 'The one you dropped!'

'I did drop a stitch,' said Kitty, 'but I soon picked it up again!'

Teddy and Billy looked at each other. It did not make sense!

'All this wool!' Kitty went on. 'I can make the scarf I was knitting into a pullover for Woody!'

But Teddy and Billy never did find out about the dropped stitch!

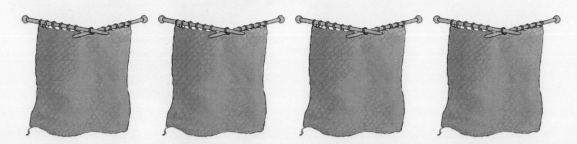

READ THESE WORDS AGAIN!

never	asked
dropped	stitch
gasped	rubbing
already	indoors
mending	undone
pulling	another
picked	looked
each	sense

WHAT CAN YOU SEE HERE?

knitting

socks

garden

pullover

wool

THE RAINY DAY PICNIC

It was a warm, sunny day. The animals were going on a picnic! There were apples for Peggy Pig, corn for Hetty Hen, carrots for Donny Donkey, hay for Hector Horse, biscuits for Dinky Dog and Pixie Puppy – and lots of other food to share.

Only Guppy Goat had seen a big, black cloud in the sky. The animals had just reached the woods, when it began to rain.

'Take shelter!' cried Hector Horse.

'Bother the rain!' said Pixie Puppy. 'This picnic was going to be fun!'

Just then they heard splashing.

'Summer rain is nice and warm!' quacked Debbie Duck.

'We like getting wet!' added Drake. 'So do the ducklings!'

The ducks looked so happy that Peggy Pig was soon rolling about in mud! 'Bathe those big feet of yours, Hector Horse!' she grunted.

'Let us jump in the puddles!' cried Donny Donkey.

Dinky began splashing about.

Pixie paddled in the puddles!

They were having such fun in the rain, nobody had seen the sun coming out!

'Look!' cried Donny. 'A rainbow! That is made by the sun shining on raindrops!'

They looked up at the rainbow. The rain had made the woods smell so fresh, and it had kept the picnic food nice and cool.

'I think,' said Guppy Goat, between bites of a crusty roll, 'this is the best picnic we have ever had!'

READ THESE WORDS AGAIN!

sunny	picnic
apples	carrots
reached	rain
shelter	bother
splashing	ducklings
grunted	bathe
jump	raindrops

WHAT CAN YOU SEE HERE?

apples

biscuits

rainbow

puddles

black cloud

WOODY DRESSES UP

Woody was putting up lots of fairy lights at Bear Towers, ready for Lady Bear's garden party.

'What fun, Lady Bear!' Teena was saying. 'Will you tell Woody?'

'No need!' said Lady Bear. 'He always looks the same!'

Woody looked down at his old clothes. 'Yes,' he told himself. 'I must look smart for the party!'

On the way home, he saw an old top hat in Brian's dustbin. 'Woody!' cried Brian. 'Can I borrow your tie?'

'Yes!' said Woody. 'Can I have this top hat?'

'Take it!' said Brian.

Then Woody saw a scarf on Farmer Bear's scarecrow! 'Woody!' cried Farmer. 'Can I borrow your jacket?'

'Yes!' said Woody. 'Can I have this scarf?'

'Take it!' said Farmer Bear.

Grandpa was throwing away an old suit. 'Woody!' he cried. 'Can I borrow your hat?'

'Yes!' said Woody. 'Can I have that old suit?'

'Take it!' said Grandpa.

The day of the party arrived.

'Woody!' cried Lady Bear. 'You do look smart in your suit, your scarf and your top hat!'

Woody just stared. Brian wore Woody's tie. Farmer Bear wore Woody's jacket. Grandpa wore Woody's old hat!

'It is a tramps' fancy dress party!' giggled Teddy. 'You are the smartest bear here, Woody!'

Everyone started to laugh, even Woody. They all had a wonderful party!

READ THESE WORDS AGAIN!

garden	party
lady	looked
old	dustbin
tie	scarf
borrow	jacket
throwing	smart
fancy	giggled

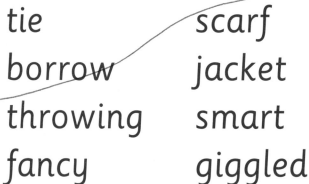

WHAT CAN YOU SEE HERE?

fairy lights

clothes

top hat

scarecrow

suit

DINKY LOOKS FOR A NAME-TAG

'I have lost my name-tag!' cried Dinky Dog. 'It was on my collar!'

'Think,' said Peggy Pig. 'Where do you remember seeing it last?'

'When I went to see Hector Horse!' said Dinky. 'Maybe my name-tag is in the stable!' So she set off.

'I have not seen your name-tag,' said Hector, 'but I found this ribbon belonging to Kitty Cat.'

'I will take it to her,' said Dinky. 'My name-tag could be at the farmhouse!' So, she set off.

Kitty was glad to have her ribbon!

'I have not seen your name-tag, Dinky,' she said, 'but I found this straw hat belonging to Donny Donkey!'

'I will take it to him,' said Dinky. 'My name-tag could be in the cabbage patch!' So, she set off.

Donny was glad to have his straw hat! 'I have not seen your name-tag, Dinky,' he said, 'but I found this bell belonging to Guppy Goat!'

'I will take it to him,' said Dinky. 'My name-tag could be in the meadow!' So, she set off.

Guppy was out in the meadow and was very pleased to see Dinky bringing his bell back.

'Thank you, Dinky,' he said.

'Now go and see Cora Cow, I think she is looking for you.'

Dinky found Cora in the cowshed. She was holding something round and shiny in her mouth and looking very pleased with herself.

'Your name-tag, Dinky! I wanted you to have it back, before you began looking all over the farm!'

READ THESE WORDS AGAIN!

lost	collar
horse	found
ribbon	belonging
house	something
meadow	pleased
looking	bell
shiny	began

WHAT CAN YOU SEE HERE?

cowshed

name-tag

cabbage patch

straw hat

stable

KNOTS IN A HANKY

Binky Bear had a habit of forgetting! He had a bath and forgot the soap! He went swimming and forgot his towel!

Then Teddy had an idea. 'Tie a knot in your hanky, Binky!' he said. 'Then you will not forget!'

Binky had forgotten his hanky, but there was one in his desk that he had forgotten about! 'What must I not forget?' he asked.

'Sports Day, tomorrow!' said Teacher Bear. So Binky tied a knot in his hanky.

'You are playing cricket!' said Teddy. 'Do not forget your bat!'

So Binky tied another knot. 'A knot for Sports Day and a knot for a bat!' he said.

'And a ball!' added Billy.

So Binky tied another knot in his hanky! 'A knot for Sports Day, a knot for a bat and a knot for a ball!' he said.

'And do not forget to bring a packed lunch!' said Teacher.

So Binky tied another knot. 'A knot for Sports Day, a knot for a bat, a knot for a ball.'

'And don't forget a knot for your packed lunch!' said Teddy.

The knots in his hanky helped Binky to remember all the things he needed for Sports Day! And his knotted hanky? That made a fine sun-hat to stop his head from getting burnt!

'Clever Binky!' smiled Teddy.

'No I am not!' said Binky. 'You told me to tie knots in my hanky so that I would not forget!'

'But it was you who did not forget to tie the knots!' said Teddy.

READ THESE WORDS AGAIN!

habit	forgetting
swimming	idea
knot	hanky
desk	sports
tomorrow	another
needed	things
remember	clever

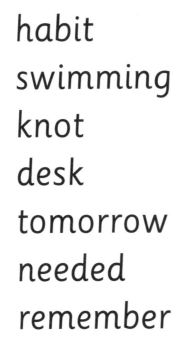

WHAT CAN YOU SEE HERE?

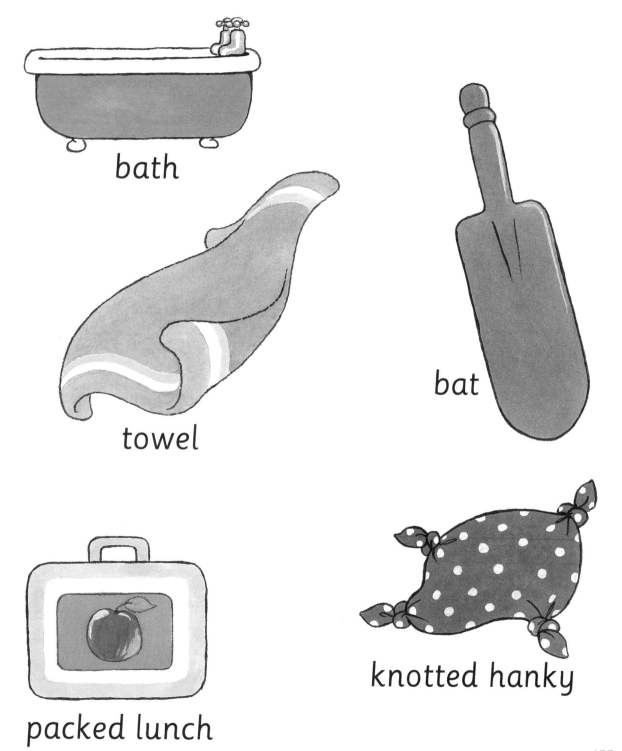

bath

towel

bat

packed lunch

knotted hanky

KITTY AND THE CAT SHOW

'Kitty Cat can be in a Cat Show at the Summer Fair!' said the farmer's wife one day.

Dinky Dog was surprised. Kitty was big and fat. Her fur was patchy and one ear was too big – not the sort of cat to be in a Cat Show! He went to tell the other animals.

'Well,' said Hetty Hen, 'Kitty IS a nice cat...'

'And she has a LOVELY purr,' said Donny Donkey.

'But she is not pretty,' said Kitten.

'I think I shall go to the Cat Show, as well!'

'We shall ALL go,' said Donny. 'Just to see what happens!'

At the Summer Fair, there were stalls with prizes to be won. There were roundabouts and swings and lucky dips, balloons and flags for everyone – and a big tent with a poster saying, CAT SHOW.

'Wait!' said Kitten. 'I must make myself look smart!' She smoothed her whiskers, washed her fur and cleaned her paws. Then they went inside.

They soon saw Kitty! She had just won a cup for being the cat with the loudest purr! Hetty, Dinky and Donny were pleased. Kitten tried to get a closer look.

'What a pretty kitten!' said a man with a camera. 'I must take her picture for my newspaper!'

Well! That made everyone VERY pleased. And Kitten? She was so happy, her purr was nearly as loud as Kitty's!

READ THESE WORDS AGAIN!

summer   fair

patchy   fur

pretty   lovely

purr   poster

whiskers   smoothed

loudest   nearly

happy   pleased

WHAT CAN YOU SEE HERE?

Kitty Cat

camera

Kitten

newspaper

balloons

TEDDY AND THE MAGIC TRICK

Everyone loved Magic Bear in his cloak and top hat. 'Close your hand!' he told Teddy. 'Now, I will tap your elbow with my wand and say – Hold Tight! All Right!'

Teddy opened his hand and there he found a bright, shiny coin!

'Again, I will tap your elbow with my wand!' said Magic Bear. 'Hold Tight! All Right! Now the coin has gone behind your ear! It is yours to keep, Teddy!'

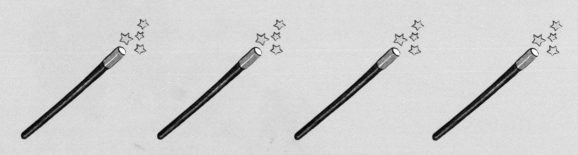

Teddy wanted to do some magic! He found a stick for a wand and a raincoat with a hood.

'I will hold my coin,' he cried, 'tap my wand and say – Hold Tight! All Right!' The coin was still in his hand!

'Some trick!' said Bella. 'Magic Bear tapped your elbow!'

So Teddy bent his arm right up.

'I tap my elbow with my wand,' he said, 'and say – Hold Tight! All Right!'

By mistake, he dropped the coin into the hood! So, when he held out his hand, it was empty!

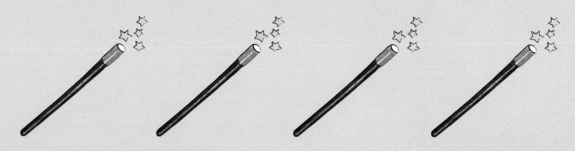

'You made the coin disappear!' said Billy. 'Now get it back!'

'I tap my elbow with my wand,' said Teddy, 'and I say – Hold Tight! All Right!' Teddy took the coin from inside his hood, then held out his hand to show them all.

'Do it again!' cried Barry.

So Teddy dropped the coin into his hood and showed them his empty hand. Then he bent his arm and took the coin out again! Nobody knew how he did it, not even Magic Bear!

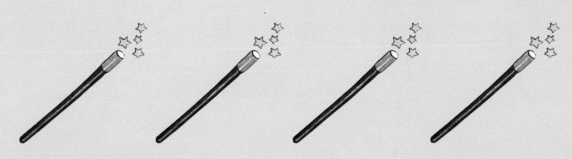

READ THESE WORDS AGAIN!

magic	everyone
tight	right
ear	shiny
stick	mistake
dropped	empty
disappear	trick
inside	again

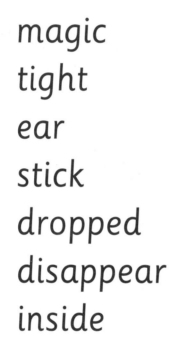

WHAT CAN YOU SEE HERE?

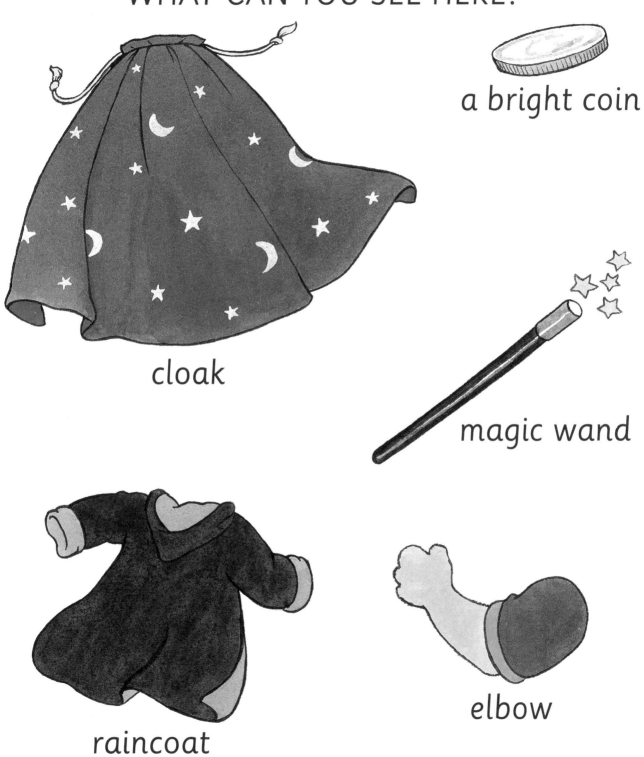

a bright coin

cloak

magic wand

raincoat

elbow

COCKEREL TRIES TO SLEEP

It had been a long, hot day.

'Get a good night's sleep, Cockerel,' said the farmer. 'We need you to wake us early tomorrow!'

Cockerel yawned. He could not sleep until the sun had set! At last, he closed his eyes.

'Ee-Aar!' sounded the alarm on the farmer's car. Cockerel woke up.

'Cock-a-doodle-doo!' he crowed.

'Quiet, Cockerel!' cried the farmer. 'Get a good night's sleep!'

Cockerel had to find a quieter place to sleep! He went to the stream and curled up under a tree.

'Quack!' said Debbie Duck. 'Do not squash my ducklings!'

Cockerel woke up. 'Cock-a-doodle-doo!' he crowed.

'Be quiet, Cockerel!' barked Dinky. 'Get a good night's sleep!'

Cockerel went to find a quieter place to sleep. He crept into the stable and curled up on the hay. A wisp of hay blew past Hector Horse. 'ATISHOO!' he sneezed. Cockerel woke up.

'Cock-a-doodle-doo!' he crowed.

'Quiet, Cockerel!' grunted Peggy Pig. 'Get a good night's sleep!'

Cockerel went to find a quieter place to sleep. He curled up in the farmyard. His eyes were just closing, when the sun began to rise.

'Cock-a-doodle-doo!' he crowed. Everybody woke up.

'What a terrible night!' said the farmer. 'Cockerel kept us awake!'

'Yes!' said Dinky. 'And you told him to get a good night's sleep!'

READ THESE WORDS AGAIN!

wake	sleep
early	tomorrow
yawned	sounded
alarm	quieter
crowed	wisp
sneezed	curled
closing	kept

WHAT CAN YOU SEE HERE?

cockerel

night

farmyard

tree

sun

TEDDY'S GOOD DEED

It was Good Deed Day in Teddy Town. First, Teddy saw Grumpy Bear trying to cross the square. 'It is Good Deed Day, Grumpy!' he cried. 'Let me take you across the square!'

'I do not WANT to go across the square!' cried Grumpy Bear. 'I was waiting for the bus!'

'Sorry,' said Teddy. Just then, Baby Bear threw a doll out of her pram! Teddy picked it up.

'It is Good Deed Day, Baby!' he said 'So, here is your doll!'

'Good deed?' said Busy Bear. 'I wanted her to throw that away!'

Teddy nearly bumped into Teena, carrying lots of shopping.

'It is Good Deed Day!' he said. 'Let me carry your shopping!'

'No, Teddy!' cried Teena. She had to run after him. 'I was only looking after Woody's shopping! Now I must carry it back!'

The next bear Teddy saw was Toy-Mender Bear, leaning on a stick!

'Poor Toy-Mender!' cried Teddy. 'Here, take my arm...'

'No!' shouted Toy-Mender Bear.

But it was too late! There was a loud CRACK and the stick broke!

'I was holding that stick for the glue to set,' said Toy-Mender Bear.

Poor Teddy!

'I only wanted to do a good deed!' he said, sadly.

'Good deed?' cried Grumpy. 'That IS a joke!'

Grumpy Bear began laughing so much that everyone forgot to be cross! Making him laugh really was the best good deed of the day!

READ THESE WORDS AGAIN!

good	deed
trying	cross
square	picked
wanted	bumped
carrying	next
crack	stick
laugh	forgot

WHAT CAN YOU SEE HERE?

bus

doll

pram

shopping

glue

GOOSE AND DEBBIE DUCK

Goose and Debbie Duck were always quarrelling!

'Your ducklings kept me awake!'

'They did not!'

'Yes they did!'

In the end, they did not talk at all. So all was quiet when poachers came to steal from the farm. They crept up on Debbie and her ducklings, meaning to steal the biggest one.

Then – HONK! HONK! Goose appeared. Her wings were spread wide and she was hissing loudly.

She pecked at the men and they began shouting.

'See those poachers off my land, Dinky Dog!' cried the farmer. 'They came up against our brave goose!'

Debbie wanted to show she was brave, too! She had an idea! If she took two goose eggs, Goose would think they had been stolen. Then, Debbie could pretend to save them!

Debbie waited for her chance. Then she took two eggs back to her nest.

'Two of my eggs have been taken!' cried Goose. 'My poor goslings!'

But Debbie was too frightened to give the eggs back! Soon, the shells cracked and two tiny heads peeped out, cheeping at Debbie.

'My goslings!' cried Goose. 'You found them, Debbie!'

Now Debbie felt more ashamed than ever, but Mother Goose was too happy to notice.

'Thank you for taking care of them, Debbie!' she said. 'We MUST be friends forever, now!'

And they were. Most of the time.

READ THESE WORDS AGAIN!

quarrelling   awake

quiet   crept

appeared   hissing

pecked   brave

idea   stolen

two   peeped

ashamed   notice

WHO CAN YOU SEE HERE?

Goose

ducklings

poachers

goslings

friends

POLICEMAN BEAR TAKES A DAY OFF

'Policeman Bear needs a day off!' said Teddy.

'He works hard!' agreed Barry.

'But who can take over?' said Binky. 'Think hard!'

A loud voice made them jump!

'Farmer!' cried Busy Bear. 'Your tractor is blocking the road!'

Farmer Bear looked a bit cross. But he soon moved his tractor!

'Thank you, Busy!' said Woody. 'I was waiting to cross!'

Then Busy saw Billy and Bella. They were playing ball. 'Hey, you two!' she cried. 'It is not safe to play near the road. Come to the park with me and Baby Bear.'

Teddy, Barry and Binky looked at each other. Then they followed Busy Bear to the park.

'We have a job for you!' said Teddy.

'A job?' cried Busy Bear. 'Oh, I DO like being busy!'

She also liked the idea of Policeman Bear taking a day off. So they all went to see him!

'You need a day off!' said Teddy firmly. 'Busy is taking over!'

'Grandpa Bear has invited you to tea!' said Busy. 'Off you go!'

Well! Policeman Bear DID enjoy his day off. And Busy enjoyed walking around, checking doors and windows and seeing bears across the road!

Now, Policeman Bear likes having a day off! And everyone likes to see him having a rest.

And, Busy Bear?

'I just like being busy!' she says.

READ THESE WORDS AGAIN!

off	over
voice	busy
road	cross
two	park
job	idea
invited	tea
enjoyed	walking
around	across

WHAT CAN YOU SEE HERE?

tractor

Busy Bear

ball

door

window

DONNY AND SAMMY SCARECROW

Donny Donkey never went far away from his friend, Sammy Scarecrow.

Late one day, the farmer and his wife went out with some friends. All was quiet. Then the sheep began bleating.

'Ted!' a man called. 'Get the sheep into the shed!'

The men got the sheep into the shed and locked the door. Then they went to fetch a truck.

'Sammy!' said Donny. 'We must stop them stealing the sheep!'

Donny pushed Sammy in his bucket towards the shed.

'How are we going to get inside,' panted Donny.

'Kick that loose plank in the shed wall and push me inside,' said Sammy.

The sheep bleated. But when they saw Donny, they were quiet.

'The sheep are quiet!' said Jim. 'We can get them in the truck!'

They went in and saw the tall shape of Sammy Scarecrow! Behind him, Donny brayed and stamped and kicked up dust.

'How did that monster get in?' cried Jim. 'We locked the door!'

'Time we were off!' cried Ted.

Out they ran, shouting and yelling, just as the farmer came home! 'Robbers!' he shouted. 'What has scared them?' He went to see.

'Look!' he said. 'Donny kicked in the loose plank to get inside the shed! But how did Sammy get inside?'

'Donny must have pushed him,' said his wife. 'We always knew that Sammy was his friend!'

READ THESE WORDS AGAIN!

never	friend
quiet	bleating
called	fetch
loose	inside
pushed	panted
monster	shape
scared	robbers

190

WHAT CAN YOU SEE HERE?

sheep

shed

scarecrow

plank

bucket

BUSY BEAR'S BABY

Busy Bear liked being busy. She also liked telling everyone what to do and how to do it!

'It is no use weeding when the sun is out!' she told Daddy Bear.

'That is quite the WRONG way to hold a cricket bat!' she told Teddy. 'You will never hit the ball like that. Let ME show you how to do it properly!'

'That Busy Bear!' moaned Daddy.

'That Busy Bear!' groaned Teddy.

'That Busy Bear!' said Mummy. 'She is putting her baby in a Baby Show! It is all she talks about!'

It was true. 'My baby MUST win the Baby Show,' Busy Bear kept saying. 'Then I shall have a party!'

Busy Bear cleaned her house, ready for the party! She even painted the flowerpots on her windowsill!

Soon it was time to get Baby ready. When she lifted him up, Busy Bear screamed!

'My baby has red spots on his face!' she cried. 'Is it Measles?'

'Heat rash!' said Mummy Bear. 'Or it could be chicken pox.'

'Send for the doctor right away!' said another bear.

Teddy felt something drip on his head. He looked up.

'It is paint!' he cried. 'Red paint!'

Busy Bear stroked Baby's chin. 'Teddy is right!' she said, looking up at the flowerpots, then looking at her baby again. 'No Baby Show for you, baby!' she said at last. 'You need a nice bath, instead!'

READ THESE WORDS AGAIN!

quite	wrong
groaned	moaned
show	true
kept	cleaned
house	ready
screamed	right
nice	instead

WHAT CAN YOU SEE HERE?

baby

face

paint

flowerpots

windowsill

POOR PEGGY PIG!

Poor Peggy Pig! The wind had blown a hole in her sty!

'Oh, dear!' she said. 'I must find a new home!' So she set off.

'I need a new home!' she told Dinky Dog. 'Can I come in your kennel?'

'Sorry,' said Dinky. 'You are MUCH too big!' Poor Peggy Pig!

On she went to the farmhouse.

'Do not bother me, Peggy!' said Cook. 'I must find a lost kitten!'

Poor Peggy Pig! 'I need a new home!' she told Hector Horse.

'Can I come in your stable?'

'No!' said Hector. 'You smell!'

'I smell like all other pigs!' Peggy said. 'YOU smell too!'

'Yes,' said Hector, 'but I smell like other horses!'

Poor Peggy Pig! On and on she went, looking for a new home. It grew dark. Then she saw a door and the glow of two tiny eyes.

How glad Peggy was to go in and lie down! She felt so hot and so very, very tired.

'Peggy!' cried the farmer next day. 'What HAVE you done? One, two, three...' he counted.

'Four, five, six...' said Dinky.

'Seven, eight, nine,' counted Hector, 'TEN fine piglets!'

'Clever Peggy Pig!' cried the farmer. 'How did you find your way inside this old trailer?'

'MEW!' mewed the kitten.

'Well, well!' said the farmer. 'Now I must make a new sty for you and your ten piglets!' And he did!

Clever Peggy Pig!

READ THESE WORDS AGAIN!

wind	sty
hole	house
kitten	stable
smell	new
two	eyes
tired	mewed
clever	inside

WHAT CAN YOU SEE HERE?

pig

kennel

farmer

horse

piglet

TEDDY AND THE SCHOOL PLAY

'We are having a school play!' said Teddy.

'How nice!' said Mummy. 'What part are you playing?'

'That is a secret!' said Teddy. 'Toy-Mender Bear is making my costume!' He said no more.

'I hear Teddy is in the school play!' said Baker Bear. 'Is he busy learning all his words?'

'No,' said Mummy. 'So, he cannot have anything to say.'

'All Teddy told ME,' said Teena, 'was that he had to make noises!'

'Noises?' said Baker Bear.

'Nothing to say?' said Mummy.

'Toy-Mender Bear making his costume?' said Daddy.

Policeman Bear frowned. 'I must look into this,' he said.

Everyone came to the play! Bella was the queen, Billy, the king, Barbara, the princess, Binky, the miller's son, and Barry, the crafty old wizard.

Then, someone else appeared!

It was someone in a furry black costume with pointed ears, fine whiskers, a long tail and a very loud 'PURR!' and 'MEOW!'

'Puss in Boots!' someone cried.

They all cheered! Clever Puss in Boots, the magic cat who helped the miller's son to beat the wizard and marry the princess!

But the best part was when Puss took off the mask which Toy-Mender Bear had made.

'Teddy!' everyone cheered as they saw his face. 'Good old Teddy Bear!'

READ THESE WORDS AGAIN!

school	play
secret	busy
words	anything
noises	frowned
everyone	king
queen	furry
purr	boots
cheered	face

WHAT CAN YOU SEE HERE?

costume

princess

Puss in Boots

wizard

mask

HECTOR'S EXCITING DAY

Hector once saw a parade of people with flags and policemen on horseback. He thought it was so exciting!

'I shall be in a carnival next week!' a police horse told him.

'How exciting!' said Hector.

'My brother is a racehorse!' said the horse. 'The prizes he has won!'

'How exciting!' said Hector.

'My uncle is in the circus,' said the horse. 'He has been on T.V.'

'How exciting!' said Hector. 'Just one exciting day would suit me!'

'Hector!' cried the farmer. 'Look at your hoof prints on my new path!'

Without thinking, the farmer took a step forward. Too late! His leg got stuck! 'Help!' he cried. 'Help!'

Off Hector galloped to get help. He saw the shepherd and Dinky Dog leading the sheep to the meadow.

'Dinky!' cried Hector. Dinky looked up. The sheep spread out. The shepherd blew his whistle. He wanted Dinky to round the sheep up again.

The sheep rushed forward, nearly knocking Hector over!

Off he galloped into a field. The moment he stopped, he heard the sound of distant music. As he walked on it got louder and louder.

'TWANG! TWANG!' came the sound of a guitar. 'BANG! BANG!' went a drum. 'HURRAH!' cheered a crowd.

There was a pop concert in one of the farmer's fields.

The noise was too much for Hector. He galloped off. The day had been much too exciting for him!

READ THESE WORDS AGAIN!

parade   horseback
exciting   prizes
suit   galloped
forward   shepherd
whistle   knocking
noise   field
crowd   concert

WHAT CAN YOU SEE HERE?

hoof
prints

flag

circus

guitar

racehorse

TEDDY AND GRIZZLE BEAR

'Grizzle Bear,' said Teddy, 'is ALWAYS grizzling at school!'

'Boo-hoo!' Grizzle grizzled, all day long. 'I want to go home!'

'If only she smiled!' said Teacher Bear. 'She might forget to grizzle!'

'Let us try!' said Teddy. 'I am tired of Grizzle grizzling!'

Billy Bear put on a funny mask.

'Go away!' Grizzle grizzled.

Barry Bear tried to give her a balloon. 'Boo-hoo!' Grizzle grizzled. 'It may go bang!'

'Let us look in the toy box!' said Teddy at last. 'Come on!'

Still grizzling, Grizzle took out a toy. 'I dropped my hanky in the toy box!' she grizzled. 'Boo-hoo!'

Teddy put his hand inside. He could not reach. He leaned over the top. Still he could not reach. He leaned a bit more, and – bump! Teddy fell inside!

Somehow, he stood up, with the box over his head.

'Ha-ha!' giggled Grizzle Bear. 'Funny Teddy Bear!'

Teacher helped Teddy out of the box. Grizzle was giggling so much, all the class giggled too!

'So, Teddy made you smile, Grizzle!' smiled Teacher Bear. 'Do you want to go home now?'

'No!' said Grizzle. 'Do some more funny things, Teddy!'

'Not now!' smiled Teacher. 'It is time for a story!'

Teddy was pleased about that. Making Grizzle smile had been very hard work!

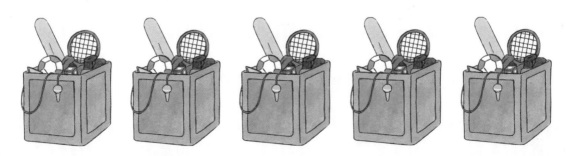

READ THESE WORDS AGAIN!

grizzle	try
tired	away
toy	bang
come	still
could	bump
helped	giggled
story	work

WHAT CAN YOU SEE HERE?

funny mask

balloon

toy box

Grizzle
Bear

Teacher
Bear

THE PUMPKIN PATCH

The farmer's wife was proud of her pumpkin patch! 'My first pumpkins!' she said. 'Just look!'

Dinky Dog and Donny Donkey had watched the pumpkins grow. Now each one was big and round and a lovely orange colour.

'A pumpkin grows so big!' said Dinky.

'Bigger than an onion,' said Donny.

'LOTS bigger than a tomato!' said Dinky.

The bigger the pumpkins grew, the more wasps buzzed around.

'Wasps!' said the farmer's wife. 'I wish I could get rid of them!'

Still the wasps buzzed, until Dinky could stand it no longer.

WHACK! She slapped her paw at a wasp. It buzzed away. SLAP! Donny hit out at a wasp buzzing around a pumpkin. SPLAT! The pumpkin broke. He hit out again. SPLAT! Another pumpkin in bits!

WHACK! Dinky hit out again. SPLAT! Donny trod on a pumpkin! WHACK! Another pumpkin broke, and another. All the pumpkins were soon in pieces!

'What will the farmer's wife say?' said Dinky at last.

'Donny!' came a voice. 'Dinky! What have you done?'

'Well..' Dinky began.

But the farmer's wife held up her hand and smiled.

'You have saved me the job of picking the pumpkins!' she cried. 'And I do not have to cut them up ready to cook! Well done! You shall have some pumpkin pie!'

READ THESE WORDS AGAIN!

wife	patch
watched	orange
colour	bigger
buzzed	longer
broke	another
pieces	saved
picking	ready

WHAT CAN YOU SEE HERE?

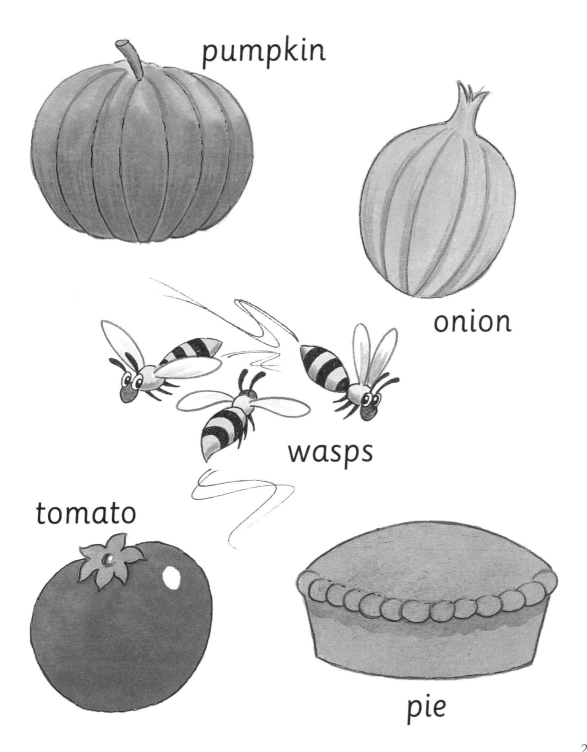

pumpkin

onion

wasps

tomato

pie

PRESENTS FOR CHRISTMAS

Teddy Town is very busy at Christmas time! Wood-Cutter Bear cuts lots of Christmas trees. Baker Bear bakes lots of cakes. Then there are presents to give!

'Teddy, please take a Christmas pudding to Grandpa Bear,' said Mummy. 'Billy can go with you!'

Billy and Teddy liked Grandpa. They went to his little house and Teddy knocked at the door.

'Here is a present for you, Grandpa!' said Teddy.

Grandpa smiled. But he sounded sad. 'I wish I had a present for you, Teddy,' he said.

Teddy did not know what to say. He turned away. Teena was across the road, looking all around.

'What do you want?' he called.

'Holly,' said Teena. 'But I cannot find any over here.'

'Plenty in my garden!' smiled Grandpa. 'Help yourself!'

Teena was pleased. She liked holly!

'Take all you like!' said Grandpa. 'My holly bushes need cutting!'

Teddy and Billy had an idea! They helped Grandpa to write a notice and tied it to the gate.

TO ALL MY FRIENDS.
HELP YOURSELVES TO HOLLY.
MERRY CHRISTMAS FROM
GRANDPA BEAR.

So many bears came to see Grandpa that Teddy and Billy had to help pick the holly!

'Merry Christmas, Grandpa Bear!' said Teena. And everybody joined in. 'Merry Christmas! Merry Christmas!'

READ THESE WORDS AGAIN!

Christmas	time
presents	trees
house	knocked
smiled	sounded
around	garden
bushes	idea
notice	tied
everybody	joined

WHAT CAN YOU SEE HERE?

Baker Bear

Christmas tree

Christmas pudding

holly

gate

SILLY GIDDY GOOSE!

Giddy Goose was so vain!

'See my fine feathers!' she kept saying. 'Look at my lovely long neck! Oh, what a fine goose I am!'

The animals took no notice. They pretended to be busy, saying good night to Cockerel!

'Good night Cockerel!' said Hetty Hen and Mother Duck.

'Good night Cockerel!' added Dinky Dog. 'You are a fine bird!'

Giddy did not like this one bit! She was just as fine as Cockerel!

Then she noticed his bright green tail feathers gleaming in the light. Just the feathers for a fine bird!

Giddy waited until Cockerel closed his eyes. Then she crept up and pecked out one, two, three bright green feathers.

'What is that?' cried Cockerel. 'Is Fox about, looking for a fine bird to eat?'

Giddy giggled. Silly Cockerel, thinking she was Fox! She tucked the bright green feathers into her wing.

'How *fine* I look!' she said.

Fox was on the prowl that night.

He had seen those three bright feathers!

'Those bright feathers mean a fine supper for me!' he cried, jumping out.

Giddy went stiff with fright! Then, there was a loud hiss and a flash of wings. Mother Goose was hitting out and pecking at Fox!

'Ow! Ow!' howled Fox, and ran off, far away from the farm!

'Silly Giddy!' said Mother Goose. 'You do not need bright tail feathers! But I do not think Fox will be coming back tonight!'

READ THESE WORDS AGAIN!

vain	lovely
notice	pretended
bright	gleaming
pecked	three
giggled	tucked
prowl	light
stiff	fright